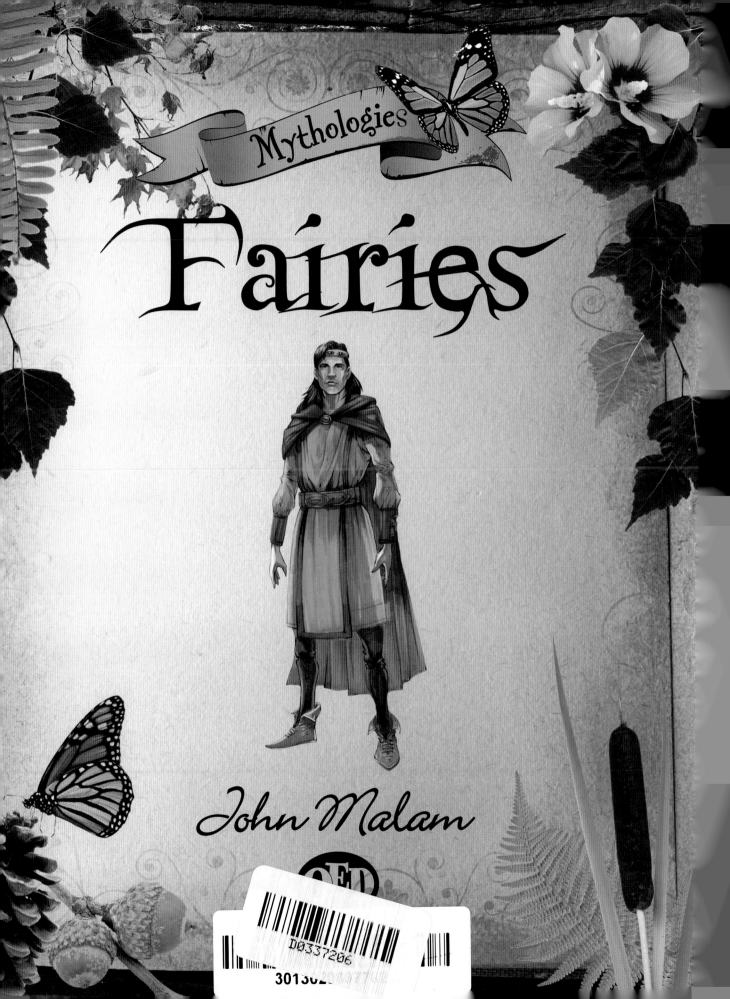

Mythologies

Fairies

John Malam

QED

Author John Malam
Editor Amanda Learmonth
Designer Lisa Peacock
Illustrator Fernando Molinaro

Publisher Steve Evans
Creative Director Zeta Davies
Managing Editor Amanda Askew

Printed and bound in China

Words in **bold** are explained
in the glossary on page 30.

CONTENTS

The world of fairies

For as long as anyone can remember, stories have been told about shy creatures we call fairies, or sometimes **fays.** It's thought that these magical beings live alongside humans in a secret world all of their own. Some fairies live in **clans**, or groups, but many prefer to live alone.

➤ *We generally think of fairies as beautiful, kind beings.*

Be careful what you say
Some believe it is unlucky to say the word 'fairy'. For this reason, it's thought wiser to call them 'little folk', 'good neighbours' or 'hidden people'.

All fairies look like humans, but they have powers that no human can ever hope to master. These timid creatures are rarely seen, but when they come into the world of people, strange things happen. Some fairy folk are good and help the humans they meet, but there are others who love to play tricks and make nuisances of themselves.

Who's who in fairyland?

Brownies
These are helpful fairies that often live in human homes where they do useful work.

Gnomes
These fairies live in the earth where they guard great treasures.

Goblins
These are bad-tempered, ugly fairies that live in dark places and make trouble for humans.

Dwarfs
These hard-working fairies live underground and help humans when it suits them.

Elves
Light elves are friendly, kind fairies, but dark elves play tricks on humans.

Hobgoblins
Although similar to goblins, hobgoblins are not as mischievous.

Nymphs
These fairies live among rivers, seas, trees, meadows and mountains.

Pixies
Similar to elves, pixies do good and bad things to humans.

5

Once upon a time:
How the Nereids saved Jason

• GREECE

This myth comes from...

The Clashing Rocks

The Clashing Rocks were found in the Bosporus Strait, a narrow passage of water with high rocks on either side. It joins the Black Sea to the Sea of Marmara, in modern-day Turkey.

➡ *The Bosporus Strait is a narrow passage of water where the Clashing Rocks were said to be found.*

In a land far away, a ram's fleece hung from a tree. It was a skin like no other, for it shimmered with gold.

There came a time when Jason, a prince of Greece, set out to take the Golden Fleece. It seemed an impossible task, as he faced many dangers, but the gods were on his side. The golden treasure soon fell into Jason's hands.

On the voyage home to Greece, Jason had to sail between the Clashing Rocks. Many a ship had been crushed by these deadly rocks, but Jason's good fortune continued. The Nereids, who were the fairies or nymphs of the sea, rose up from beneath the waters and lifted his ship to safety. After this, the nymphs returned to their secret home under the sea, ready to guide other sailors to safety.

➡ *The Nereids lifted Jason's ship onto the crests of the waves, safely beyond the reach of the deadly Clashing Rocks.*

NEREIDS

The **Nereids** were the daughters of the sea god Nereus. There were 50 Nereids, all of whom were young and beautiful. They rode through the sea on creatures called **hippocamps**, which were part-horse, part-fish.

Fairies that live in troops

Fairies are similar to humans in many ways. Just like people, some fairies live together in communities or clans.

These are called **trooping fairies** and they like nothing better than to troop or parade in colourful processions, with lots of dancing, feasting, singing and music. They are ruled over by kings and queens, and each year they celebrate the great festivals of **Beltane** and **Samhain**.

➡ *At the festival of Samhain, fairies sing and dance, watched over by the king and queen.*

⬇ *All that's left of this burial mound in Ireland is the stone chamber inside it, where a person was once buried. Today, it's said to be the home of the Little Folk.*

The most famous trooping fairies live in Ireland, British Isles. They are the Daoine Sídhe (say: *deena shee*) or Little Folk, who live in and around the country's ancient **burial mounds** and lonely thorn trees. Daoine Sídhe fairies are tall and thin, with beautiful faces, sweet voices and long, flowing hair.

The blood that flows through their veins is pure white. They try to remain out of sight of humans, but if disturbed they make bad things happen. Humans suddenly fall ill and farmers' crops mysteriously die. Worst of all, babies are stolen and fairy babies called **changelings** are left in their place.

However, the Little Folk do have a good side. Humans who are unwell leave them gifts of food, hoping the fairies will use their magic to heal them.

fairy festivals

In the world of fairies, there are two seasons – summer and winter. The festival of Beltane (1 May) marks the start of summer, and the festival of Samhain (31 October) is the start of winter.

Changelings

A changeling is a fairy baby swapped for a human baby. This can only happen if the human baby has not been **baptized** (given its name in a religious ceremony). If the human parents discover it is a fairy baby, the changeling will vanish and the human child will be sent home alive and well.

◄ *If a human family is left with a changeling child, the infant cries constantly and grows up into a weakling.*

9

Once upon a time:
The girl who dances with a fairy king

• IRELAND

This myth comes from…

Fairy protector

In Ireland, British Isles, Finvarra is known as the protecting spirit of the family. This is because he once returned a kidnapped woman, Etain, safely to her home. If humans are kind to him, he rewards them with good harvests and fine horses.

➡ *The young girl danced and danced with King Finvarra.*

There was once a young girl who was loved by Finvarra, king of the Irish fairies. Every night the fairies came to her house and led her away to dance with the king.

The more she danced, the more she wanted to live with the Little Folk forever. Then, as night became day, they vanished, and she awoke in her bed.

One day, she told her friends what happened to her at night. They said she must have been dreaming, but the girl said it was all true. To prove it, she would show the fairies to them.

That night, she took her friends to where the fairies met, but as it was dark and cold they grew frightened and ran back to their homes. The girl was left to wait on her own. The fairies came, and as she danced the night away she wished to be with them forever.

The fairies granted her wish and her spirit passed from the human world into the fairy world. From then on, she lived among the Little Folk. If you know where to look, you might see her dancing with King Finvarra.

← *Finvarra, the kind-hearted king of the Irish fairies.*

→ *This hill at Knockmaa, County Galway, Ireland, is said to be King Finvarra's home.*

Fairies that live alone

Some fairies spend their entire lives on their own. They are called **solitary fairies**. They want to be left alone either because they are terribly shy, or because they find it hard to get along with other fairies.

Whatever the reason for living alone, these fairies are always connected with particular places, such as the homes of humans, woodlands or ancient burial mounds.

Solitary fairies can be complete opposites. Some, such as brownies, are helpful and kind towards humans. Others, such as goblins, can be mischievous. A human family should hope that a brownie comes to live with them in their home, not a goblin. For a small reward, such as a bowl of fresh milk left out at night, a brownie will work while humans sleep.

◄ *A goblin in the house means one thing — trouble!*

In the morning, the humans will wake to find the house magically cleaned from top to bottom. However, if a goblin moves in, the household chores will be left undone. Instead, this unwelcome guest will spread dust, break plates, hide things and make a mess.

▲ *Morgan le Fay was a magician as well as a fairy. Here, she brews a potion while she says a magic spell.*

Changing their shape

Some solitary fairies are shape-shifters – they can change into creatures of beauty, hideous beings or even become invisible. Morgan le Fay (the Fairy) is a shape-shifter who can change into a bird and fly away.

▲ *Spilled milk is a gift for the fairies.*

Spilled milk

Milk is a favourite drink of all fairies. If any is spilled by a human, it should be left where it falls as a gift for the fairies. It should never be cleaned up because the fairies will think their present is being taken from them.

Once upon a time:
The fairy who changed shape

• ENGLAND

This myth comes from…

⬇ *Robin Goodfellow loved to play tricks on lost travellers.*

One moonless night, a group of men were crossing a dark, lonely heath, somewhere in England.

A mischievous hobgoblin lived on the heath, and he watched as the men tried to find their way home. The **sprite** was Robin Goodfellow who, though he was good by name, was not always good by deed. He played tricks on people, as the travellers were about to discover.

Robin Goodfellow went up to the men and offered to show them the way. Thinking they had found a true friend, the men set off after him. As they followed their guide, Robin Goodfellow shifted his shape. The hobgoblin changed into a **will-o'-the-wisp** – a strange, flickering light that made him look like a walking fire.

Night light

At night, balls of light can sometimes be seen glowing low over swamps and marshes. They are known as will-o'-the-wisps. They are probably caused by natural gas from rotting plants catching fire.

↑ *Will-o'-the-wisps are also known as foolish fire, as travellers often mistake them for lights in houses.*

Wherever he went, the men went, too. Up the heath and down it, all night long. Only when the first rays of sunlight appeared was the spell lifted. Robin Goodfellow sent the weary men on their way with the sound of his laughter ringing in their ears.

Shakespeare's fairy play

In William Shakespeare's play 'A Midsummer Night's Dream', Robin Goodfellow plays the part of a fairy called Puck. There are other fairies in the play, including Oberon and Titania, the king and queen of the fairies.

➡ *This painting shows Puck, who faces us, near the middle, from Shakespeare's 'A Midsummer Night's Dream'.*

Mischievous elves

A race of magical creatures lives in the colder countries of northern Europe. In Denmark they are called 'ellen', in Germany 'alfar', in Sweden 'elvor' and in Britain they are called elves.

These fairies all look like miniature humans – elf men are always ugly, elf women always beautiful. They make their homes in dark forests, often in hollowed-out tree trunks or ancient burial mounds.

⬆ *Elves live deep in the forest in secret, hideaway places.*

⬇ *A prehistoric flint arrowhead, or 'elf arrow'.*

Elf arrows

Thousands of years ago, human hunters used arrows with points made from pieces of flint. In parts of Europe, some people used to call them elf arrows.

BLAME IT ON ELVES

Elves get the blame for many things.

- If you have knots and tangles in your hair, you have elf locks.
- Plants and trees twisted out of shape are known as elf twisted.
- A strange fire at night over a swamp or marsh is an elf fire.
- If a person suffers a mysterious illness they have an elf shot.
- Another word for a birthmark is an elf mark.

The elf race can be divided into elves that live above ground (light elves) and those that live underground (dark elves). Light elves are friendly, but dark elves are not.

◄ *A twisted, knotted tree is thought to be the work of elves.*

Dark elves cast spells over humans that last for years. They steal milk and bread, and will swap their own babies for human children. A human family tricked into bringing up an elf child will suffer years of misery.

Once upon a time:
Rip Van Winkle and the elves

• USA

This myth comes from…

Rip Van Winkle was a man who lived in a village at the foot of the Catskill Mountains, USA. One day, he went hunting in the woods near his home.

As evening drew near, Rip began his journey home. On the way, he met a small man with a long beard and bushy hair. He was dressed in old-fashioned clothes and was carrying a heavy barrel of wine. He was an elf.

The elf asked for help, so Rip took his barrel and followed him to a clearing where there were other elves, all playing ninepins. The elves drank the wine – and so did Rip. Before long, he fell fast asleep.

➡ *The mischievous elves cause Rip Van Winkle to sleep for 20 years.*

When Rip woke up, the sun was in the sky. Thinking he had slept the night on the mountain, he hurried home, but his village seemed different. A crowd gathered to look at the stranger, and when Rip told them his name, he was met by puzzled looks. Rip Van Winkle, they said, had left the village 20 years ago, and had never been seen from that day to this.

← *The story of Rip Van Winkle was written in 1819 by American author Washington Irving.*

➡ *Ninepins is an older version of skittles and bowling.*

The game of ninepins

Ninepins is similar to the modern games of bowling and skittles. Nine bottle-shaped pins are arranged in the shape of a diamond. Wooden balls are rolled to knock the pins down.

Gruesome goblins

If it's knee-high to a human, always grumpy and has an ugly, wrinkled face, it's probably a goblin. These unpleasant creatures spell trouble for humans. Some live as **house fairies** and make nuisances of themselves.

Goblins only come out at night, when they love to cause mischief.

Hello to a hobgoblin

If you had to choose between a hobgoblin and a goblin in the house, pick a hobgoblin. It's just as ugly as a goblin, but hairier, and will be helpful rather than harmful.

Goodbye to a goblin

The only way to rid a home of a goblin is to scatter flax seeds on the floor. He won't have time to pick up all the tiny seeds before dawn, which will really annoy him! If you do the same over the next few nights, the goblin will get so fed up, he'll leave the house.

House goblins enjoy making floorboards creak, rattling handles, knocking on doors and snatching bedclothes off sleeping people. It's no wonder that humans often think their house is haunted by a ghost.

Not all goblins spend their lives in the homes of humans. Some are found in human workplaces, especially underground places such as mines. Others lurk under rocks or among the twisted roots of ancient trees.

➡ *Scattering flax seeds on the floor is a good way to get rid of a goblin.*

Once upon a time:
The goblins who live underground

• BOHEMIA

This myth comes from…

Deep inside the mountains of Bohemia, in central Europe, lies a great treasure. Locked within the ancient rocks is a precious store of silver ore, the raw material of silver coins and jewellery. For hundreds of years, miners have dug into the mountains, as if they were rabbits burrowing into hills.

At the silver mines of Kutná Hora, a town in the Czech Republic, workers tell tales of mine spirits they call Wichtlein (Little Wights). These underground goblins look like little old men with long beards. They are dressed as miners and they carry lanterns, mallets and hammers.

KNOCK, KNOCK

The tin mines of Cornwall, England, are also said to be home to noisy goblins. They are known as Knockers, as the sound of knocking could often be heard from deep within the mine.

⬆ *Tin mines like this one in Cornwall are believed to be home to goblins called Knockers.*

As the miners work, small stones rain down on them. This, so they say, is the work of the goblins. The goblins also guide the miners to the silver. They knock from inside the rock to tell the miners if they are close to the ore. However, the knocking can also signal danger – three loud knocks warns a miner that he is about to die.

◄ *The goblins of Kutná Hora use axes to knock from inside the rock, guiding miners to the silver.*

Gifts for goblins

The Wichtlein goblins expect to be brought gifts of food every day. If not, they will take their revenge by showering the miners with more stones.

Once upon a time: Rumpelstiltskin

This myth comes from…

• GERMANY

O nce there was a man who boasted to a king that his daughter could spin straw into gold. It wasn't true, but the king believed the man and ordered the girl to make him some gold.

Left alone at her spinning wheel, the girl began to cry. Her sobbing reached the ears of a dwarf, and that night he called on her. The dwarf promised to spin the straw into gold, in return for the girl's necklace. The king was delighted with the gold, but he was greedy and wanted more.

That night, the dwarf returned and spun more gold, and in return the girl paid him with her ring. Again, the king demanded more, and the dwarf came and did his magic a third time. As the girl had nothing left to give the dwarf, a bargain was struck. She agreed to give the dwarf her first child.

Rumpelstiltskin was a dwarf who could spin straw into gold.

The importance of names

Names are important in stories about fairies. If a human baby is not baptized, it is un-named. This means it is at risk of being snatched by fairies. Also, calling out the name of a fairy is believed to be a way of making it appear.

The girl married the king, and after a year she had a child. One night, the dwarf came to take the baby, but the girl refused.

The dwarf said that she could keep the infant only if she could discover the dwarf's name. Messengers travelled the land to find out. In one place, they overheard a curious little man gleefully calling out his name and saying he was soon to take a human child.

The dwarf returned, and when the girl said his name was Rumpelstiltskin, the evil creature cried out in rage and stamped so hard that he tore himself in two and died.

27

Fairy magic

If there's one thing above all that fairies are famous for, it's magic.

When a **milk tooth** falls out, you probably put it under your pillow at bedtime and hope for a visit from the **tooth fairy**. A **fairy godmother** might make good things happen to you – but only as long as you believe in the magic of fairyland.

▲ *Fairies are said to meet inside toadstool rings.*

Circles of ancient stones or rings of toadstools are said to be magical places where fairies meet. A human that joins fairies inside a fairy ring crosses over from this world into a mysterious place where strange things happen.

FAMOUS FAIRY GODMOTHER

In the much-loved fairy tale of Cinderella, a servant girl's life is changed forever thanks to her fairy godmother. The young girl changes into a rich woman, and she is freed from her hard-working life.

➡ *The Fairy Godmother used her magic to help Cinderella go to the prince's ball.*

Fairy magic makes the human invisible to other humans, and they lose all sense of time. A few hours spent dancing in a fairy ring may turn out to be many human years.

Fairies cast their magic over humans in many ways. Even though they don't exist in real life, they will always live inside our imaginations. Fairy stories have been told for hundreds of years, and will continue to be told for many more.

A photo of Frances Griffiths with her paper fairies, taken by Elsie Wright. After more than 60 years, the girls (who were then old ladies) finally admitted that their fairies weren't real.

fairy fakers

In 1917, two girls made paper cut-outs of fairies and took pictures of them in their garden. Elsie Wright and Frances Griffiths, from Bradford, England, told people they had seen real fairies, and many people believed them.

GLOSSARY

Baptize
To give a child its name during a special Christian ceremony known as a baptism.

Beltane
An ancient festival held on 1 May to mark the start of summer.

Burial mound
An ancient mound of soil placed over the burial place (grave) of a dead person.

Changeling
A fairy baby swapped, or changed, for a human baby.

Clan
A group of fairies that all live together.

Elf arrows
The name given to arrow heads made from pieces of flint. They were made thousands of years ago, but before that was known, it was thought they were made by elves.

Fairy godmother
A kind fairy who helps and protects a human as if the person was their own child.

Fay
Another word for fairy.

Hippocamp
In the myths of ancient Greece, a sea creature that was part-horse, part-fish.

House fairy
A fairy that lives in a human's house, where it usually does helpful work.

Milk tooth
A tooth in the first set of a baby's teeth.

Nereids
In the myths of ancient Greece, the Nereids were a group of 50 nature fairies.

Samhain
An ancient festival held on 31 October to mark the start of winter.

Shape-shifter
A fairy that can change shape from one thing to another.

Solitary fairies
Shy, secretive fairies that live alone, and always stay close to their homes.

Sprite
A general word used to describe any type of fairy.

Toad-stone
A stone that people thought lay inside toads. The stone was worn as a lucky charm, as people believed it would protect them from harm.

Tooth fairy
A fairy that leaves a gift, such as money, under a child's pillow when one of the child's milk teeth falls out.

Trooping fairies
Fairies that live in clans, or groups, and like to march, or troop, in processions.

Will-o'-the-wisp
A ball of fire, seen at night, that moves close to the ground over moors and heaths.